Get set... GO!

Cheese

Judy Bastyra

Photography by Michael Michaels

Contents

About cheese	2	Toasted cheese hearts	14
10 golden cooking rules	4	Quick spinach lasagna	16
		Cheese biscuits	18
Cheese spread	6	Mini cheese cakes	20
Cheesy bacon salad	8	Party dinosaur	22
Cottage cheese lamb	10	Index	24
Cheesy fruit lollies	12		

Watts Books

London • New York • Sydney

Fife
COUNCIL
King's Road Primary School
Rosyth - Tel: 313470

About cheese

Cheese comes in many different colours and textures.

Soft cheeses are good for mixing, spreading and baking. They are good in salads, sandwiches and cakes.

fromage frais   *curd cheese*   *cream cheese*   *cottage cheese*

Hard cheeses are good for grating, melting and shaping.

parmesan

cheddar

edam

Blue cheeses have a
very strong flavour
and are good for
salads and dressings.

stilton

Danish blue

<small>HOW TO GRATE CHEESE</small>

✔ Cut a lump of cheese bigger than
the amount you need.

✔ Put the grater on a board
to catch the grated cheese.

✔ Hold the cheese at one end.

✔ Always grate downwards.

10 golden cooking rules

✔ Wash your hands  before you begin.

✔  Read the whole recipe carefully.

✔ Make sure you have all the ingredients and equipment you need.

✔ Measure out the ingredients carefully.

✔ Allow at least 15 minutes time for the oven to warm up.

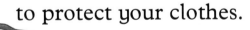

✔ Wear an apron  to protect your clothes.

✔ Use a separate spoon if you want to taste the mixture.

 ✔ Always use oven gloves
to put something in the oven and to take it out.

✔ Always turn the handle of
a saucepan on the stove to one side.

✔ Finally, don't forget to do the washing up!

GUIDE TO THE MEASUREMENTS USED
tbl/tbls – *tablespoon/s*   tsp/tsps – *teaspoon/s*
g – *grams*   ml – *millilitres*

 Wherever you see this symbol,
it means that you should
ask for help from an adult.

Cheese spread

Get ready

- ✔ 50g hard cheese, grated
- ✔ 100g cream cheese
- ✔ 1 small onion, grated
- ✔ Half a carrot, grated
- ✔ 1 celery stick, chopped
- ✔ Salt and pepper
- ✔ Mixing bowl
- ✔ Fork

...Get set

Put the hard and soft cheese in a bowl.
Mash them together with a fork.
Mix in the onion, carrot and celery.
Season with salt and pepper.

 **Go!**

Spoon the spread into a small pot.
Use it as a sandwich filling
or try it grilled on toast.

Cheesy bacon salad

Get ready

✔ 50g Cheddar cheese   ✔ Cucumber   ✔ 1 tsp sugar

✔ 50g Danish blue   ✔ Radishes   ✔ Half a tsp mustar

✔ Lettuce, washed   ✔ 2 cooked   ✔ 5 tbls oil

✔ Tomatoes   bacon rashers   ✔ 2 tbls vinegar

✔ Salt and pepper   ✔ Knife   ✔ Jam jar with lid

...Get set

Put the lettuce in a bowl.

Cut the tomatoes into quarters.

Slice the radishes and cucumber.

Cut the cheese and bacon into small pieces.

Add all the ingredients to the bowl.

≈≈≈ Go!

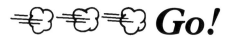

Shake the oil, vinegar, sugar and mustard togethe
in the jam jar with the lid screwed on tight.
Pour the dressing over the salad.

Cottage cheese lamb

Get ready

✔ 2 hard boiled eggs   ✔ Cottage cheese   ✔ Knife
✔ 4 dates   with pineapple   ✔ Plate
✔ Cucumber   ✔ Radish   ✔ Spoon

...Get set

Cut one egg in half longways to make the head.
Cut the other in half across and remove the yolk.
Use half the white to cut the sun's rays and the ear
Cut a thin circle from the rest for the sun.

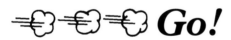 **Go!**

Spoon the cheese on to the plate
to make the lamb's body.
Add the egg head, ear and sun and dates as legs.
Slice the cucumber to make grass
and trees with radish centres.
If you like, add a small piece of date as an eye.

Cheesy fruit lollies

Get ready

✔ 2 tubs of fruity fromage frais, such as strawberry and banana

✔ Small pieces of fruit

✔ 4 flat lolly moulds and sticks

✔ Knife

...Get set

Put the lolly sticks in the moulds
Fill each mould with fromage frais.
Level the cheese off with a knife.
Add the fruit pieces on top.

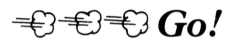 **Go!**

Carefully put the moulds into the freezer.
Take them out after two hours.
Dip them into warm water
to remove the lollies from the moulds.

Toasted cheese hearts

Get ready

- ✔ Sliced bread
- ✔ Small tomatoes
- ✔ Plain paper
- ✔ Margarine
- ✔ Hard cheese, grated
- ✔ Small knife
- ✔ SET THE GRILL TO HIGH

...Get set

Draw a heart shape on the paper.
Cut it out and use it as a pattern
to cut hearts from the bread slices.
Toast the bread hearts
under the grill on one side.
Spread margarine on the other side.
Top with the grated cheese.

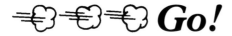 Go!

Grill the cheese-topped hearts for 5 minutes.
Decorate with the tomatoes cut in half.

Quick spinach lasagna

Get ready

- ✔ 1 tbl oil
- ✔ 1 onion
- ✔ 225g frozen spinach, thawed
- ✔ 1 tbl cream
- ✔ Salt and pepper to taste
- ✔ Pinch of nutmeg
- ✔ 1 box non-cook lasagna
- ✔ 50g hard cheese, grated
- ✔ Ovenproof dish
- ✔ Knife
- ✔ Frying pan
- ✔ SET THE OVEN TO 180°C/350°F/GAS MARK 4

...Get set

Cut the onion into small pieces.
Fry it in oil for 5 minutes.
Add the spinach, cream, salt, pepper and nutmeg

 **Go!**

Make alternate layers in the dish
of cheese, pasta, spinach, pasta and cheese.
Top with grated cheese and bake for 45 minutes.

Cheese biscuits

Get ready

- ✔ 250g plain flour
- ✔ A pinch of salt
- ✔ 100g margarine
- ✔ 2 egg yolks
- ✔ 50g grated cheese
- ✔ 2 tbls tomato sauce
- ✔ 1 whole egg, beaten
- ✔ Rolling pin
- ✔ Bowl
- ✔ Biscuit cutters
- ✔ Baking tray
- ✔ SET THE OVEN TO 200°C/400°F/GAS MARK 6

...Get set

Rub the margarine into the flour and salt.
Stir in the egg yolks and grated cheese.
Add the tomato sauce and form into a ball.
Roll the dough out on a floured surface
till it is about 1 cm thick and cut it into shapes.

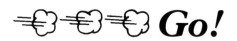 **Go!**

Put the shapes on an oiled baking tray.
Brush the tops with the beaten egg.
Bake for 12 minutes and then leave to cool.

Mini cheese cakes

Get ready

- ✔ 6 digestive biscuits
- ✔ 50g melted butter
- ✔ 225g caster sugar
- ✔ 225g curd cheese
- ✔ 2 eggs
- ✔ Lemon juice
- ✔ Wooden spoon
- ✔ 2 bowls
- ✔ Paper cake cases
- ✔ Patty tin
- ✔ Fruit to top
- ✔ SET OVEN TO 160°C/300°F/GAS MARK 2

...Get set

Crush the biscuits in a bowl
till they make fine crumbs and add the butter.
Put a layer of biscuit mixture in each paper case.
Press it down firmly with the back of the spoon.
Mix the eggs, sugar, cheese and lemon together.
Spoon on to the biscuit layer to fill the cake cases.

═❀═❀═❀ Go!

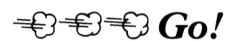

Put the paper cases in the patty tin.
Bake for 25 minutes. Top with fruit and chill.

Party dinosaur

Get ready

✔ 1 pineapple   ✔ 1 kiwi fruit   ✔ Wooden toothpicks

✔ Hard cheese, cut   ✔ 2 raisins   ✔ Knife

    into triangles

...Get set

❗ Cut the leafy top off the pineapple.

Cut a slice from the length of the fruit as the tail.

❗ Scoop the flesh out of the centre of the rest.

Cut it into cubes for later.

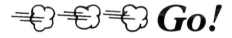 **Go!**

Peel the kiwi and cut out the mouth.
Stick on raisin eyes using toothpicks
and a tongue cut from a pineapple leaf.
Thread pineapple cubes and small triangles
of cheese on to toothpicks and stick into the body
Add the tail and large cheese triangles as spines.

Index

blue cheese 3

cheddar cheese 2
   8
cheese biscuits
   18–19
cheese cakes
   20–21
cheese spread 6–7
cheesy bacon
   salad 8–9
cheesy fruit lollies
   12–13
cottage cheese 2,
   10

cottage cheese
   lamb 10–11
cream cheese 2, 6
curd cheese 2, 20

Danish blue 3, 8

edam 2

fromage frais 2,
   12

grated cheese 3,
   6, 14, 16, 18,

hard cheese 2, 6,
   14, 16, 22

parmesan 2

soft cheese 2, 6
spinach lasagna
   16–17
stilton 3

toasted cheese
   hearts 14–15

First published in 1995 by
Watts Books
96 Leonard Street
London EC2A 4RH

Franklin Watts Australia
14 Mars Road
Lane Cove
NSW 2066

Editor: Pippa Pollard
Design: Ruth Levy
Cover design: Shoba Mucha
Artwork: Ruth Levy

Special thanks to Charles
Bradley, assistant food designer
and stylist.

A CIP catalogue record for this
book is available from the
British Library

Dewey Decimal Classification:
641.6

UK ISBN 0 7496 1497 8

10 9 8 7 6 5 4 3 2 1

© 1995 Watts Books

Printed in Malaysia

King's Road Primary School
Rosyth - Tel: 313470